Title: Tomahawks and Trombones

Author: Barbara Mitchell

This book misrepresents what happened when pilgrims and Native Americans interacted. Also does a poor job of representing Native Americans.

Tomahawks and Trombones

Tomahawks and Trombones

by *Barbara Mitchell*
pictures by *George Overlie*

Carolrhoda Books • Minneapolis, Minnesota

To my mother and father for
Christmas, their Great Day

LIBRARY OF CONGRESS CATALOGING IN PUBLICATION DATA

Mitchell, Barbara, 1941-
Tomahawks and trombones.

(A Carolrhoda on my own book)
Summary: Relates how a group of Moravians, living in
Bethlehem, Pennsylvania, around 1755, used heavenly music
to defeat the Delaware Indians.
  1. Moravians—Pennsylvania—Bethlehem—History—Juvenile literature. 2. Bethlehem (Pa.)—Siege, 1755—Juvenile
literature. 3. Delaware Indians—Wars, 1750-1815—Juvenile
literature. 4. Pennsylvania—History—French and Indian
War, 1755-1763—Juvenile literature. [1. Moravians—History. 2. Bethlehem (Pa.)—Siege, 1755. 3. Delaware Indians
—Wars, 1750-1815. 4. Indians of North America—Wars,
1750-1815] I. Overlie, George, ill. II. Title. III. Series.

F159.B5M56   974.8'22   81-21661
ISBN 0-87614-191-2   AACR2

        1 2 3 4 5 6 7 8 9 10 88 87 86 85 84 83 82

A Note from the Author

This story takes place in the Moravian city of Bethlehem, Pennsylvania, around the year 1755. We remember the Moravians for the faith and courage they brought to the New World. We remember them also for their music. They gave us the first orchestra in America, they gave us the famous Bach Choir, and they gave us an unusual group called the trombone choir.

Some of this story comes from a 225-year-old diary kept by the Moravian sisters. Some of it comes from a peace talk given by Bishop Spangenberg at the end of the French and Indian War. Some of it is legend. And some of it is imagined. It may not have happened exactly as it has been told, but if you read both with your eyes and your heart, you too might hear the music of the trombones.

At the foot of the Blue Mountains,
where the Lehigh River
meets the Creek with Many Bends,
was a little Pennsylvania town
named Bethlehem.
The people who lived in Bethlehem
called themselves the Moravians.
The Moravians loved God,
they loved peace,
and they loved music.

Outside the town
lived the Delaware Indians.
The Delawares fished in the Lehigh.
They built their wigwams
by the Creek with Many Bends.
They hunted in the Blue Mountains.
The Delawares loved peace too.

The Moravians were like
one big family.
They called each other
"Brother" and "Sister."
They lived in groups called choirs.
Each choir had its own house.

And each had its own work to do.
The single sisters' choir
lived in The Sisters' House
on Sisters' Lane.
They did spinning and weaving,
and they took care of the children.

The single brothers' choir
lived in The Brethren's House
down the hill.
Their house was full of workrooms.
They made everything
that Bethlehem needed.
The married couples' choir
lived in The Family House.
Some of them worked in Bethlehem.
Others went out to teach
the Delawares.
Children had their own choirs.
There was a boys' choir school
and a girls' choir school.
The children's work was learning.

13

But no matter what work they did,

everyone in Bethlehem sang.

Sisters sang weaving songs

to make their work go faster.

Brothers sang working songs

to help them hammer harder.

Families sang songs at breakfast

to start the busy day.

Even the watchman sang a quiet song

to put the town to sleep.

Many Moravians
also played instruments.
When the first Moravians
came to the New World from Europe,
each family could bring
only one sea chest.
But tucked into the chests
were violins and flutes,
oboes and French horns.
One instrument, though,
would not fit: the trombones.
So, sadly, the Moravians left
their trombones behind.
And there were no trombones
in the New World yet.

Bethlehem had a music-master.

His name was Brother Johann.

One summer day, Brother Johann

looked out his window.

The fields were full
of golden wheat.
The air was full of music.
The people of Bethlehem
were on their way to harvest.
Sisters marched in one long line.
Brothers marched in another.
They were all singing.
The miller was playing his flute.
Even the town's leader,
Bishop Spangenberg,
marched along with his violin.
"If only we had trombones,"
Brother Johann thought.
"Harvest is a time for trombones."

The next day,

he went to see the bishop.

"Bishop Spangenberg," he said,

"do you remember the trombones?

Bethlehem is 12 years old now.

It's time we had trombones."

The bishop remembered.

Trombones playing from church tops.

Trombones playing from castle tops.

Trombones at harvest.

Trombones on Easter morning.

Trombones on *Christmas* morning.

Christmas was the Moravians' Great Day.
They started getting ready for it
in the fall,
when the brothers made hundreds
of little beeswax candles.

On Christmas Eve,

everyone went to the church

for Love Feast.

They sang the Christmas hymns

and shared buns and coffee together.

Then they lit their candles

and carried them out

into the cold, dark night.

And in the Old World,

at dawn on Christmas day,

trombones had played

the Christmas Chorale.

Yes, Bethlehem needed trombones.

"We shall order them from Germany,"

the bishop said.

The Moravians had a big new ship.

It was called the *Peace*.

The next time she sailed,

the *Peace* carried a message:

Bethlehem needs one set of trombones.

Brother Johann waited all fall.

He waited all winter.

He thought about trombones.

He thought about who would play them.

"Brother Peter—the soprano for him.

Brother Andrew on the alto.

Brother David will play the tenor.

And I will play the bass."

Brother Johann built himself

a tall trombone chair.

One spring night,

the watchman sang a special song.

"Ship's in! Ship's in!

Cargo for Bethlehem!"

Brother Johann hurried outside.

There were four long boxes.

The trombones!

In the morning, Brother Johann
called his players together.
They began to practice.
They practiced and practiced.
By summer, they were playing hymns.
And by Christmas,
they could play chorales.

Very early on Christmas morning,
they climbed to the roof
of The Brethren's House.
The Christmas Chorale
sounded out over Bethlehem.
The music was beautiful.
The trombones sounded
clear and strong.

The people in Bethlehem
were filled with joy.
"Oh!" they said. "Listen!
Trombones for Christmas!
How we have missed them!
How fine the New Year will be
with trombones for Easter
and trombones for harvest!"

But the New Year, 1755,
was not so fine.
Stories of Indian attacks
filled the air.
French settlers and English settlers
both wanted all the fur trade
in the New World.
Each side took more and more land
away from the Indians.
They pushed the Indians
off their best hunting grounds.
The Indians got angrier and angrier.
They began to attack
the settlers' homes.

In July,
the French and Indian War began.

The Moravians had paid the Delawares
for their land.
They had welcomed the Delawares
in their town.
Many Delawares and Moravians
had become friends.

But people no longer saw each other
as people now.
They saw only red skin or white skin.
And in the fall,
the crops were poor.

There had been no rain.

The Delawares had almost no corn.

Fur trappers were taking
their animals.

The Delawares were starving.

A tribe called the Iroquois
laughed at them.
"You are weak," they said.
"You have let the white man
take all you have.
And you call these Moravians
your friends."
Finally even the peaceful Delawares
could stand no more.
They began to burn barns and houses
all around Bethlehem.

One day close to Christmas,

the governor's men came to Bethlehem.

"You should all leave," they said.

"It is not safe to stay here."

"Leave Bethlehem?" asked the brothers.

"Not have Christmas in Bethlehem!"
cried the sisters.

They all turned to the bishop.

Bishop Spangenberg bowed his head.

At last he spoke.

"We will stay," he said.

"Bethlehem will watch and pray."

The brothers built

tall, log watch-towers.

They boarded up the windows.

The bishop sent for Sister Anna.

"Sister," he said,

"I am sending sleds into the country

to gather all the children.

You can expect 300 children

for Christmas Love Feast."

Three days before Christmas,
a friendly Indian
banged on the bishop's door.
He had been running all night.

"The Indians plan to attack Bethlehem
by your Great Day!" he said.

The brothers kept watch day and night.

"I want Bethlehem kept very quiet,"

said the bishop.

Brother Johann looked at Brother David.

Trombones were not quiet.

Would there be no trombones

this Christmas?

At last it was Christmas Eve.

But nobody could go to the church
for Love Feast.

The clock ticked away.

Nine o'clock . . . ten o'clock . . .
eleven o'clock . . . twelve o'clock . . .
one o'clock . . . two o'clock.

At three o'clock,

Sister Anna peeked outside.

She saw Brother Peter go off watch.

Then Brother Andrew.

Then Brother David.

Brother Johann followed.

They walked right up the middle
of the empty street.

"How dangerous!"
Sister Anna said to herself.
She watched them knocking
on the bishop's door.

"What are they up to?"
she wondered.

The clock struck four.

The brothers on watch

heard noises down by the creek.

Indians were crouched

all along the bank.

The brothers picked up their rifles.

This is it, they thought.

Suddenly a loud sound
cut through the air.
It was clear and strong.
It was beautiful.
The Indians had never heard
anything like it.
The music echoed
off the stone houses.
It filled the morning sky.

The Indians were frightened.
"Music up in the sky!" they said.
"It must be the voice
of the Moravians' God!

Surely He watches over this place."
They lowered their tomahawks
and walked quietly back
into the woods.

The children heard the music too.

"Trombones!" they shouted.

"It's Christmas!"

Everyone ran to the church.

There would be Love Feast after all.
But for this one year,
it would be on Christmas morning
instead of Christmas Eve.

The sisters passed baskets of buns.
The brothers passed mugs
of creamy coffee.
Everyone sang.
The bishop lit the first candle.
Soon the room glowed
with hundreds of little lights.
The children did not know
that Indians had hidden
all night in their woods.
They only knew that
it was Christmas in Bethlehem.

Afterword

Did the trombones

make the Indians go away

on that Christmas day?

No one really knows.

But according to legend,

a Delaware later told a sister

it was the strange music in the sky

that made them lower their tomahawks.

And even now,

trombones play a message of peace

each Christmas in Bethlehem.

Mitchell,Barbara,
    1941-

    Tomahawks and trombones